CONTEMPORARY ACCORDION

Oak Publications
New York • London • Sydney

CONTEMPORARY
ACCORDION

Dedication
To Kate—I dedicate this book to my loving wife. It is together that we pursue our lives in music and although this work is of my pen, her opinions, enthusiasm, and general influence in my music are represented here.

Special thanks
to Arlene, Jason, Peter, and the Oak staff, to Art Friedman for my first fiddle tune on the accordian, to Michael Schlesinger for the extensive use of his records, and for the use of their records, Don Kent, Jim Garber, Pate Conte, Art Friedman, and to the folks at Arhoolie, Philo, Shanachie, Folkways.

Disclaimer
Despite an exhaustive search, we have not been able to locate the publishers or copyright owners of several of the compositions and photographs. Therefore, we have proceeded on the assumption that no formal copyright cleaims have been filed on these works. If we have inadvertently published a previously copyrighted composition without proper permission, we advise the copyright owner to contact us so that we may give appropriate credit in future editions.

PHOTOGRAPHS

David Frazier	9, 10, 12, 13
Donald Sullivan	18
Herbert Wise	26
Country Music Foundation Library and Media Center Nashville, Tennessee	43
David Moss	50
Edmund Shea	62
Nelson Allen	74
Unknown	77
Paul Dovell	80
Elliot Landy	86
Diana Davies	95
Donaa Leiserowitz	Back Cover

edited by: Patricia Ann Neely
Cover design by: David Nehila
Book design by: Katrina Orlowsky

©1981 Oak Publications
A Division of Embassy Music Corporation, New York
All Rights Reserved

International Standard Book Number: 0-8256-0240-8
Library of Congress Catalog Card Number: 80-84767

Exclusive Distributors:
Music Sales Corporation
257 Park Avenue South, New York, NY 10010
Music Sales Limited
8/9 Frith Street, London W1V 5TZ England
Music Sales Pty. Limited
120 Rothschild Street, Rosebery, Sydney, NSW 2018, Australia

Printed in the United States of America by
Vicks Lithograph and Printing Corporation

Table of Contents

Preface

Since the middle 1800's the accordion has filled many taverns and dance halls with zesty music and has become a major folk instrument in the western world. This book will give you transcriptions and a little insight into the accordion as a folk instrument. Its purpose is to serve as an instruction manual for the intermediate musician, a material source for the advanced player, and an anthology of the most noted folk accordion styles of the United States, Canada, Ireland, and England. The tunes range from easy to advanced and a special section is included on left-hand technique for the pianist or other keyboard person interested in playing accordion. The accordion is a portable instrument and is a good one for people interested in playing at street corner jam sessions, festivals or just learning a new instrument. This book is written for the piano type keyboard. In order to use it you must be able to read standard music notation and have a working knowledge of the piano type keyboard.

Foreword

There has long been a need for a comprehensive folk style accordion book. In recent years revivalists have been recording and writing about ethnic music for many instruments including guitar, banjo, fiddle, penny whistle, and mandolin. The accordion also has its place in folk music. Just as the banjo, the accordion has long been a great companion of the fiddle in ethnic dance music. It can provide a strong rhythmic drive and can create a lively and very exciting tune.

Several types of accordions as well as many musical styles used are discussed in this book. All have different advantages. The full size 120 bass piano accordion can be played easily in all keys having more than three octaves of treble keys, major, minor, seventh, and diminished chords, as well as single note bass buttons. A button accordion has buttons on the right side instead of piano type keys. Diatonic button accordions sound different tones when you pull or push the bellows. Good staccato can be achieved with your bellows as well as with your fingers. Many accordion players today have piano accordions and you can purchase one second hand for a reasonable price. It is the folk tradition to use whatever instruments are available.

This book is concerned with accordion music of Ireland, England, the United States, and Canada. It was not long after its invention in the early 1800s in Europe, that the accordion became popular in England and Ireland. It is one of the few folk instruments which can play a different melody, rhythm, and bass at the same time. Although the accordion stands up well on its own it has the ability to blend nicely with other instruments. Instrumentation in Irish music can range from solo to large or small ensembles. In Irish group music you may find accordion, fiddle, tin whistle, mandolin, flute, or tenor banjo in any combination playing the melody together in an ensemble. Piano is generally a rhythm instrument along with guitar and bodhran (an Irish drum). Writers have been trying for years to put Irish music on paper, but have found it best to encourage learning by listening to the music.

Many English, Irish, and Scottish settlers who came to America found their way into the secluded Appalachian and Ozark mountains before the invention of the accordion. Their strong European background became the seeds which rooted the tradition of southern mountain music. Had timing been different, I'm sure the accordion would have found great sounds in the southern mountains. For those who came later, a small instrument such as the fiddle, was much more practical on the frontier. The accordion has always been an expensive instrument and unlike many wooden instruments nearly impossible for even a handy frontiersman to construct. However, it has a festive pride and managed to survive extinction to become a major folk instrument along the Mexican border, Cajun country (Louisiana bayous), and the New England states. The German settlers and the Hohner company were, for the most part, the force behind the two row button accordion in southern Texas. The traditional music of this area is called Norteno' music. German influence can be heard in Norteno' polkas and mazurkas. Flaco Jimenz is a Norteno' accordion player of both traditional and contemporary music. Through the Ry Cooder Band, Flaco is helping to popularize Norteno' music throughout America.

A fusion of Cajun music and blues from the Mississippi River area has produced the most interesting sounds in blues accordion. Clifton Chenier is widely recorded and is one of the best Cajun blues (Zydeco) accordion players. Good, traditional Cajun accordion music can be heard on Nathan Abshire and Joe Falcon's recordings.

A typical band in the French Canadian Provinces or in the New England area would include fiddle, accordion, spoons, and piano, or guitar. The fiddle generally plays the melody and the piano or guitar supplies the rhythm. The accordion does both. French Canadian tunes adapt well to the piano accordion. I have transcribed some tunes from Jean-Marie Roberge and Philippe Bruneau, who is a master of the single and three row button accordions.

The accordion is also quite enjoyable when used as a backup instrument in vocal tunes. Many cowboy bands in the 1940s used the accordion. Gordon Fleming tastefully backs up Alan Mills singing songs of the maritimes. In fact if you look hard you can find the accordion behind anyone from Bill Monroe and the Bluegrass Boys (Sally Ann Forrester) to Bob Dylan and The Band (Garth Hudson).

I quit the accordion at age 13 after about five years of formal lessons and went on to play organ with several rock bands in the late 60s. I spent two years playing guitar, bass, mandolin, and accordion with a New York old-time string band called the Wonderbeans, *Wonderbeans* (Flying Crow FC 101). I am presently performing with my wife and we're simply known as Kate and Lou, *Kate and Lou* (Flying Crow FC 105). If you were like me, an accordion dropout, take the old case out of the cellar, dust it off, and help put the accordion back into the spotlight. Play some good accordion music. If you've been faithful all along I hope this book will give you some new tunes, some insight into folk style accordion, and many happy hours. Enjoy.

Louis Giampetruzzi

Introduction
Free Reed Instruments

The accordion is only one in a family of free reed instruments. When you push or pull the bellows, you force air through a hole in which a metal reed is attached on one end and vibrates on the other. Different size reeds produce different tones.

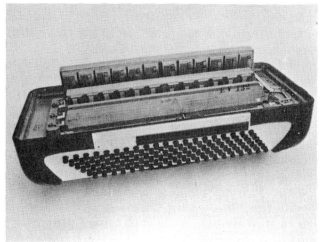

Other free reed instruments

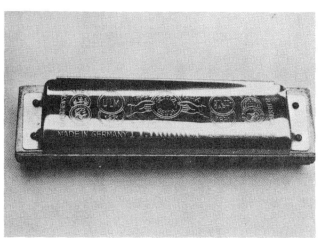

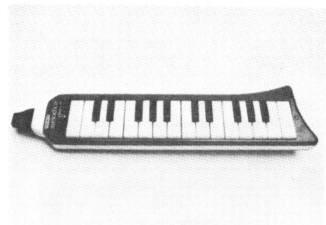

Listening

There is a lack of good folk style piano accordion on record. Because of this shortage it is important to listen to recordings of other instruments to find various examples of good material and to get new musical ideas. In bluegrass, the guitar developed and moved primarily from a rhythm role to a well respected lead role in the past quarter of a century. In jazz, the saxophone has had a steady development from the 1930s through the 1950s. Now it's the accordion's turn.

What to Listen For (a five-fold listening plan)

1. Listen to as much piano accordion music as you can. Clifton Chenier and Johnny Handle (the High Level Ranters) are good places to start.
2. Listen to other free reed instruments such as button accordion, concertina, and harmonica and listen to tunes in which the free reed sound has already been successful.
3. Fiddle tunes of any genre adapt well to the accordion. I have found fiddle music to be my wealthiest source for material.
4. Listen to piano and organ music for licks that are successful on the piano type keyboard especially in blues and jazz.
5. Don't limit yourself. Listen to several types of instruments and the various styles in which they are played. It is surprising to find how good a mandolin, guitar, or clarinet break may sound on the accordion.

Right-Hand Technique

Most folk instruments have one thing in common. Once you've learned some basic techniques you should be able to play basic tunes. Character and subtlety tend to be more important than complexity or precision.

Scales and Fingering—ascending

Most of the tunes in this book stay within the boundaries of their own key and scale. When you play an ascending scale on the accordion remember to finger down toward the floor. After fingering three or four notes your thumb should slip under your other fingers, enabling you to continue your range to the limit of the fingerboard.

C-scale—ascending

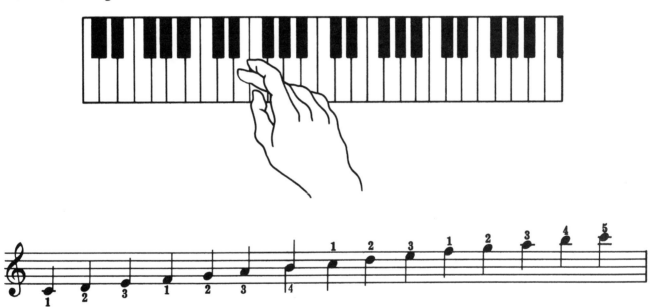

Scales and Fingering—descending

When playing a descending scale on the accordion remember down in pitch is fingering away from the floor. After fingering three or four notes your middle or your ring finger should pass over your thumb enabling you to continue your range to the limit of the keyboard.

C-scale—descending

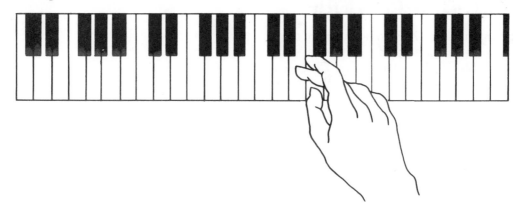

D-scale

Hand Positioning

Quite often you will come across a tune which does not have an easy flowing stream of notes. This may mean skipping across the keyboard and back. When this occurs it is helpful to separate a line of music into shorter phrases.

Example: "Flop-Eared Mule" (pg. 34)

I separate the first line in "Flop Eared Mule" into three phrases and three hand positions.

phrase 1

phrase 2

phrase 3

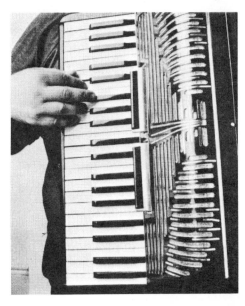

To change your hand position in a flowing sequence of notes you will quite often have to play a note with one finger and shift to another finger on the same note.

Exercise

Left-Hand Technique

Most accordion players past the beginner level probably have this section mastered, but take a brief look through it to be sure you understand the systems I use in this book. This section is especially for the pianist or other keyboard person interested in playing the accordion. The left-hand technique used in this book is very simple and with a little practice most anyone can master it within a few weeks.

There are 120 bass buttons on the left-hand side of the accordion. In this book we will, for the most part, use only about twenty buttons. In order to get a good perspective on the left hand, lay the accordion on a table in front of you with the buttons nearest you.

Notice: 1. There are 120 buttons, six rows of twenty.
2. Rows of six slant down to the right.
3. Either one or three buttons will be marked with an indentation, a rough edge, or a stone.

The two top rows (nearest the bellows) are single bass notes. The other four are chords.

Row 1 — Counter bass notes (nearest the bellows)
Row 2 — Fundamental or root bass notes
Row 3 — Major chords
Row 4 — Minor chords
Row 5 — Seventh chords
Row 6 — Diminished chords

The diagonal rows 3 through 6 are directly related by name to row 2 (fundamental or root note row). The first row is a relative counter bass button.

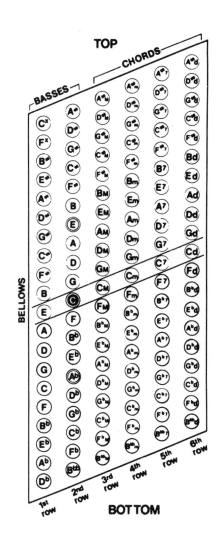

14

The center marked button in row 2 is a C note. The buttons in that diagonal row are:

Row 2 — C note
Row 3 — C Major chord
Row 4 — C minor chord
Row 5 — C seventh chord
Row 6 — C diminished chord
Row 1 — E note (relative counter bass note to C)

Pickup your accordion and place your fourth (ring) finger in row 2 on the C note button. Play this note and alternate by playing the C major chord button in row 3 with your middle finger. The chord button will be in the same diagonal row directly behind the C note. The rhythm should sound like this: um-pa-um-pa-um-pa. Practice this until it feels smooth.

To play a minor chord use this fingering:
1. Fourth (ring) finger on the C note button (row 2).
2. Index finger on the C minor chord button in row four (same diagonal row as the C note, two rows behind).
3. Practice the same rhythm (um-pa-um-pa).

This rhythm is used for $\frac{2}{4}$ or $\frac{4}{4}$ time. Another rhythm you will use in this book is $\frac{3}{4}$ or waltz time. To play a waltz bass press your C note button once and your chord button twice. It should sound like this: um-pa-pa-um-pa-pa. Practice this rhythm with the minor chord fingering too.

The buttons you will be concerned with in this book are B♭ in row 2 and the seven buttons above it. They are B♭, F, C, G, D, A, E, B. Locate these notes and their respective major chords (use the bass finder chart on pg. 14).

Left-Hand Notation

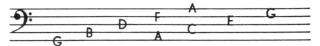

Notes below the middle line of the staff are all single notes (row 1 or 2).

Notes on or above the middle line of the staff are all chords (rows 3 through 6). One of the following letters will always appear in the notation to indicate which type chord (and which row) to play.

M — indicates a major chord in row 3.
m — indicates a minor chord in row 4.
7th — indicates a seventh chord in row 5.
d — indicates a diminished chord in row 6.

Notes with a short line underneath them are to be played in row 1.

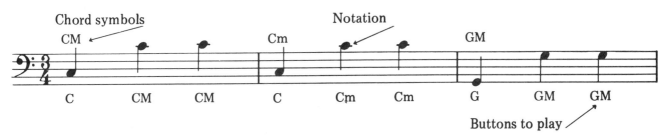

The Alternating Bass

The left-hand technique used in traditional folk tunes is called the *alternating bass*. This technique is similar to some backup guitar or piano styles. To play a C major chord with alternating bass place your:

1. Fourth finger on the C note button in row 2.
2. Third finger on the C major chord button in row 3.
3. Second finger on the G note in row 2.

Play these buttons in the following sequence: C - CM - G - CM

The C major chord with alternating bass is notated like this:

The buttons you have played are all next to each other and form a triangle. This triangle is moveable up and down the fingerboard within rows 2 and 3.

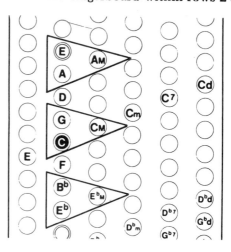

Bass Patterns

In folk music accordion players almost always use alternating bass patterns. If you have trouble reading left-hand music, memorize a few bass patterns and follow the chord symbols written above the bass notation. Always be sure to check the bass notation for bass runs. I have listed below, the chord symbols in column one, the corresponding notation in column two, and the mate bass buttons in column three. Use the bass button finder chart on page 17.

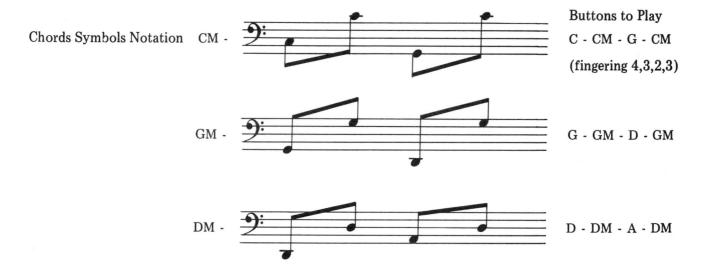

Chords Symbols Notation

CM -

GM -

DM -

Buttons to Play

C - CM - G - CM

(fingering 4,3,2,3)

G - GM - D - GM

D - DM - A - DM

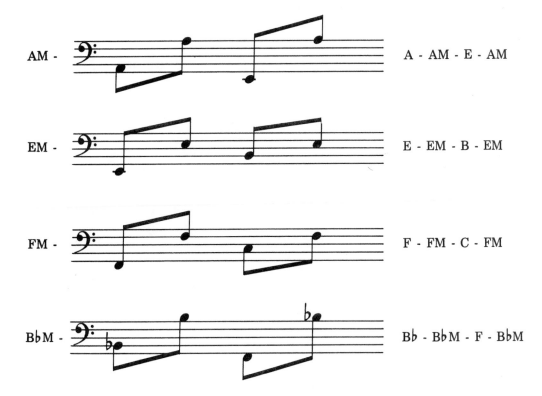

AM - ... A - AM - E - AM

EM - ... E - EM - B - EM

FM - ... F - FM - C - FM

BbM - ... Bb - BbM - F - BbM

Now you can play all the major and minor chords by simply moving your fingers up or down within the same rows. More left-hand techniques will be discussed later.

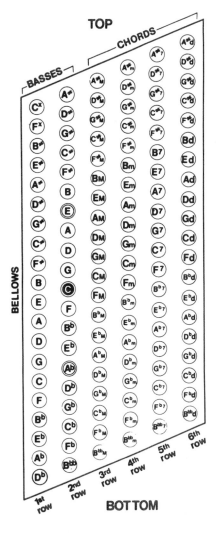

A Few Words Before Beginning

Most of the tunes discussed in this book were not developed formally in written music, but developed through the musical traditions of many people over the years. Try to put a little of yourself into each tune by playing it freely, not just note-for-note. Try playing your tunes at various speeds. It is important to be creative with your music, but when you play traditional music it is also important to have a good understanding of the music you are borrowing. Traditionalists will often dislike a modern interpretation of an old tune while some contemporary people wouldn't have it any other way. You can't please everyone, but try to understand the roots of the music you choose to play and possibilities for variation.

The Tunes

The single, most important aspect of achieving smoothness with your right hand is good fingering. The small numbers above various notes throughout the book will give you the best fingering for some of the key notes in otherwise finger-twisting passages.

Veronica and Jim McDermott of Bold McDermott Roe.

Irish and English Tunes
Morpeth Rant

"Morpeth Rant" is one of the best-known Northumbrian dance tunes. Northumbrian music orginated in the northeast of England. This tune is also in the repertoire of many American old-time musicians. I have transcribed "Morpeth Rant" from *Alan Block and Ralph Lee Smith* (Meadowlands Records MS 01). A fine button accordion version by Tommy Edmondson can be heard on *Northumbrian Country Music* (Topic 12TS267).

Triplets

This tune begins with a *triplet*. A triplet is a musical phrase of three notes and in this case is written as sixteenth notes. The time value of a triplet written in this form is equivalent to two sixteenth notes.

Morpeth Rant

Dennis Murphy's Polka

"Dennis Murphy's Polka" is a traditional tune from Kerry county, located on the southwest coast of Ireland. The music of this area is not as ornamented as most Irish music. Jimmy Doyle (button accordion player) and Dan O'Leary have recorded this tune as "Charley O'Leary's Favorite" on *Traditional Music From The Kingdom of Kerry* (Shanachie 29007). A version without accordion is on *The Chieftians II* (Island 9365).

Tone Registers

I often play Irish or English tunes with my lighter registers. Try your clarinet or piccolo registers for whistle and flute-like sounds.

Dennis Murphy's Polka

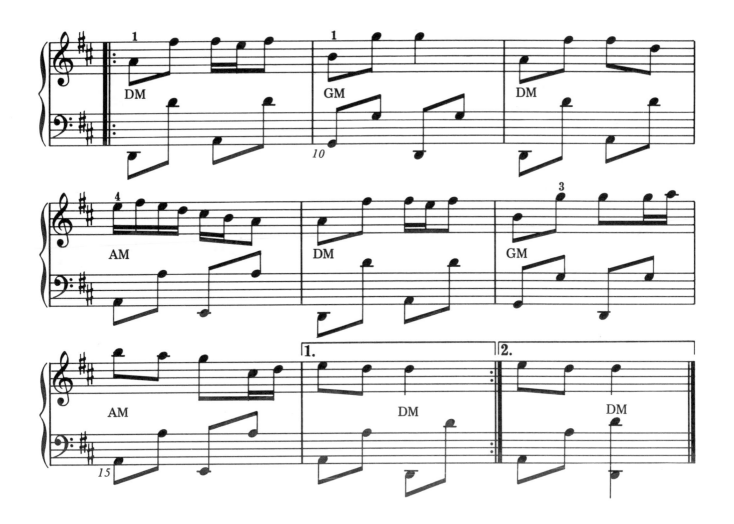

Portsmouth

This tune is played by Ian Holder on a Shirley Collins record, *Adieu to Old England* (Topic 12TS238). The melody of "Portsmouth" has all the joy of returning from sea or of a drinking good time in a waterfront tavern.

Bass Run

A good bass run whether played by a rhythm guitar player, a bass player, or your own left hand on the accordion will be a welcome addition to a tune. The bass run in measures 8 and 9 leads you from a D note and chord to a G note and chord. The line under the B note ♩ indicates that this

note is to be played in bass row 1.

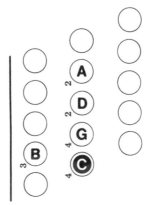

Portsmouth

The Brickmakers

This tune is from John Kirkpatrick and Sue Harris's recording, *Among the Many Attractions* (Topic 12TS295). John Kirkpatrick is one of the leading button accordion revivalists in England performing traditional music as well as blending his accordion tastefully into some contemporary English folk-rock records.

Grace Notes

Grace notes are small notes with a slash which have no time value. The grace notes in this tune can best be described as a roll. Place your thumb on middle C and play (roll) five consecutive notes quickly, accenting the last. This musical phrase should make a one syllable sound (*brrrum*).

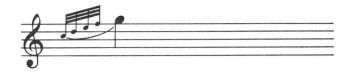

The grace notes between the first two notes can best be compared to a fast triplet with an accent on the last note.

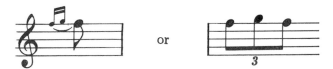

The Brickmakers

24

Neil Wayne, concertina (left) and
Bob McQuillen, accordion (right).

Dusty Bob's Jig

"Dusty Bob's Jig" is an Irish tune which I learned from Dudley Laufman and the Canterbury Orchestra, *Swinging on a Gate* (Front Hall FHR 03). This fine album features both Dudley Laufman and Bob McQuillen on piano accordion. Even though Dudley plays harmonica and Bob plays piano on "Dusty Bob's Jig," I chose it because it sounds great on the accordion. Remember, sometimes you can find interesting material in a non-accordion source.

$\frac{6}{8}$ Time

A jig is a lively dance tune played in $\frac{6}{8}$ time. In $\frac{6}{8}$ time there are six eighth notes per measure or any combination of notes equaling six eighths.

Jig Bass

When you play a steady bass rhythm in most $\frac{2}{4}$ or $\frac{4}{4}$ tunes the notes and chords are usually equal in time value (for example see "Morpeth Rant" pg. 18. The bass notes and chords are all eighth notes except for the last chord). In a jig you are confronted with putting a four-note bass pattern into a six-note rhythm. This can be accomplished by alternating quarter and eighth notes.

Dusty Bob's Jig

Harvest Home

John Handle is a leading piano accordion revivalist. I have transcribed two tunes from his recordings. The first, "Harvest Home," is a hornpipe recorded on *Welcome to Cafe Lena* (Biograph BLP 12046). A Library of Congress recording, *Reels, Polkas and More* (LBC 4) features the Margaret McNiff-Locke Trio playing this tune under the title "Brown's Hornpipe."

Staccato

Playing a note short and sharp, giving it approximately half its time value, is called *staccato*. Staccato is notated with a dot above or below the note. note.

The first two measures of the B part are good exercises for the thumb. It can be surprisingly difficult to play the same note three or four times consecutively with the same finger. Give a few extra minutes to these two measures.

Harvest Home

28

Drops of Brandy

Johnny Handle and the High Level Ranters recorded a good version of this slip jig on *Johnny Trailer* (Trailer LER 2007).

$\frac{9}{8}$ Time

In $\frac{9}{8}$ time there are nine eighth notes per measure or any combination of notes equaling nine eighths. A jig in $\frac{9}{8}$ time is called a slip jig.

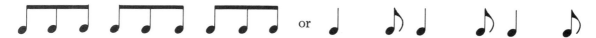

Slip Jig Bass

When playing a slip jig you are confronted with putting a six-note bass pattern into a nine-note rhythm. You can accomplish this by alternating quarter and eighth notes (see "Dusty Bob's Jig," pg. 26 jig bass for a $\frac{6}{8}$ time comparison).

Johnny Handle and the High Level Ranters

Drops of Brandy

The Humors of Westport

This reel is from an album by Joe Burke, Andy McGann, and Felix Dolan, *A Tribute to Michael Coleman* (Shaskeen OS 360). Joe Burke was the Senior All Ireland Accordion Champion in 1959 and 1960.

Ornamentation

Ornamented notes are the fanciful trills which give Irish music its distinction and beauty. The ornamentation is written in grace notes, but you must listen to Irish music in order to play these ornaments correctly. Many writers have different methods of notating ornaments but most agree that listening is the best way to get a feel for the music.

Below are two ways to play the ornaments in measures 10 and 12 of this tune.

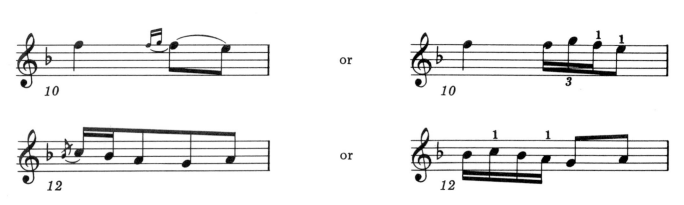

The Humors of Westport

American Tunes
Flop Eared Mule

The accordion was used most in the southern mountains as a backup instrument in gospel music (Orna Ball plays accordion on Rounder Records with her husbands E.C. Ball). Nevertheless, I have included a few southern mountain dance tunes. Traditional dance tunes usually have two or three parts. The parts are referred to as the A part, B part, and C part. See page 12 for the A part instructions for "Flop Eared Mule."

This is a good tune for strengthening the third, fourth, and fifth fingers of your right hand. Watch the fingering carefully. The note is sometimes played with your second finger and sometimes with your third. If you use the correct fingering the notes will all fall into place.

Flop Eared Mule

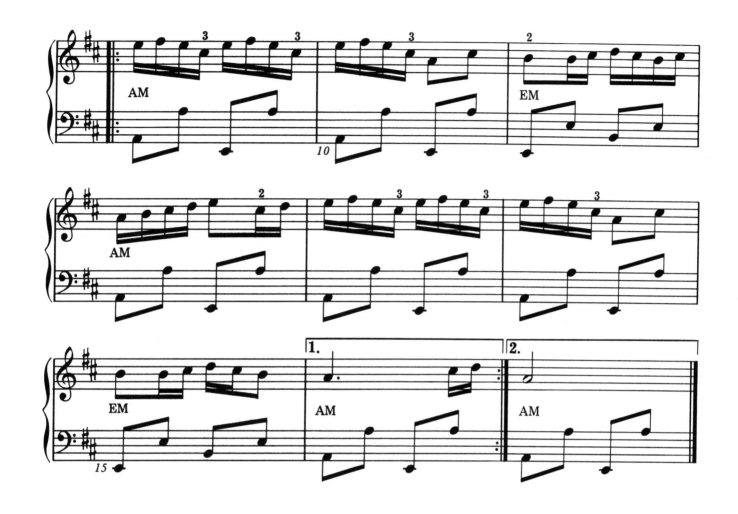

Mississippi Sawyer

This tune is played mostly by old-timey fiddlers. I learned it from an album entitled *Alan Block and Ralph Lee Smith* (Meadowlands MS 01).

Mississippi Sawyer

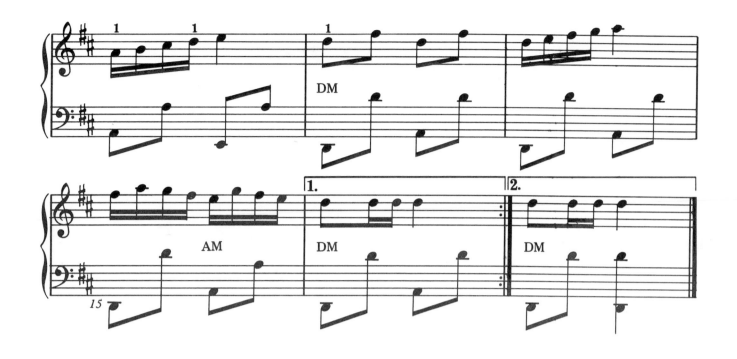

My Own House Waltz

"My Own House Waltz" can be heard on the Highwoods String Band album, *Fire on the Mountain* (Rounder 0023). Old-time country waltzes are played a little on the brisk side in the southeast.

Everlasting Joy

"Everlasting Joy" is a bluegrass gospel tune from Charlie Bailey and the Happy Valley Boys with Phyllis McCumby on accordion. I have transcribed the Phyllis McCumby introduction, some backup chords, and an adaptation of the mandolin break. (Old Homestead Records OHCS 102).

Backup

When playing backup in bluegrass, the accordion helps fill two slots. The left hand is similar to guitar backup and the right hand joins the mandolin in playing upbeat chords. The right-hand chord is played along with the left-hand chord buttons on the second and fourth eighth notes of the measure.

Inversions

You have the option of playing the right-hand chord in its most natural position, with the root note on the bottom, or in an inverted position, with a note other then the root note on the bottom.

Various D Chord Positions

Everlasting Joy

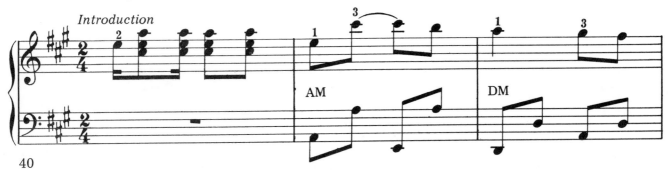

Bill Monroe and the Bluegrass Boys.

Rocky Road Blues

This is a bluegrass tune recorded by Bill Monroe and the Bluegrass Boys, *16 All Time Great Hits* (Columbia CS 1065) and yes, there is accordion on the original (Sally Ann Forrester). Sally Ann Forrester plays rhythm accordion and adds a good texture to this bluegrass tune. I have recorded this tune with an accordion break on *Kate and Lou*. (FC 105).

Blues Notes in Bluegrass

The instrumental side of Bill Monroe is clearly influenced by the blues. "Rocky Road Blues" is a 12-bar blues tune.

The Blues Scale

In a blues scale the third and seventh degrees of the scale are lowered a half tone. The blues scale in the key of A has a flatted third (C♯ becomes a C note) and a flatted seventh (G♯ becomes a G natural).

Blues Technique

Horn players can slide into some notes. Guitarists can pull strings. On accordion grace notes are often used in playing a bluesy lick. In measure 9 the grace notes give you a slide sound.

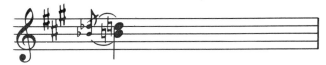

In measure 10 the double grace note coupled with the C eighth note is played like a fast sharp triplet. This is one of my favorite sounds on the accordion.

   or

Rocky Road Blues

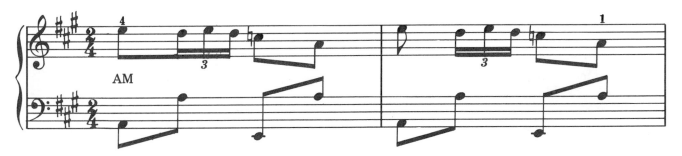

Chicken Reel Stomp

Many cowboy and western swing bands in the 1940s used the accordion. The *Beer Parlor Jive* album (String 801) catches Eddie Fielding taking the tune "Chicken Reel" in the key of D and slipping into the key of G with some good licks making it "Chicken Reel Stomp."

Parallel Run

A parallel run occurs when two notes move at equal intervals in the same direction.

Measures 11 and 12 illustrate a short run of parallel thirds. These thirds can function as a bridge linking the G chord to an E chord. Notice all the notes in measure 11 are played with your second and fourth fingers. It is sometimes easier to move your hand position than to seek different fingers for each set of notes.

In measures 26 and 27 I use only my first and third fingers for I find this type of fingering gives me a good bounce.

Chicken Reel Stomp

48

Beer Parlor Jive

Here is another tune from the *Beer Parlor Jive* album (String 801). This time it features Darrell Kirkpatrick on the squeeze box.

Circular Patterns

A circular pattern is a series of notes which repeat themselves sometimes with a slight variation. This is a good device to use when jamming on a blues progression. The break in "Beer Parlor Jive" begins with this pattern.

French Canadian Tunes
St. Anne's Reel, La Bastringue, and Le Reel du Sucre

Three D Tunes

"St. Anne's Reel," "La Bastringue," and "Le Reel du Sucre" are all D tunes. These tunes sound good as a medley as well as individually. They have some similarities in form and technique and learning three D tunes in a row should give you a good feel for that key. All three A parts start on the F# note and head toward lower notes. All three B parts head up toward a high B note.

Arpeggios

When the notes of a chord are played in a sequence rather than together this is called an *arpeggio*. I find it helpful to keep chord positions clear in mind when I play arpeggios. The B part in "La Bastringue" revolves around these two chord positions.

The B part in "St. Anne's Reel" also starts on a D chord position.

Measure 7 of "St. Anne's Reel" uses a G and A chord position.

"St. Anne's Reel" — *The Wonderbeans* (Flying Crow FC 101) — accordion.
"La Bastringue"* — *Philippe Bruneau* (Philo 2003) — button accordion.
"Le Reel du Sucre" — *Kate and Lou* (Flying Crow FC 105) — accordion.

Art Friedman, Ann Weiss, and Louis Giampetruzzi (left to right).

* "La Bastringue" is an excellent recording with button accordion player Philippe Bruneau and is in the key of C. Most fiddlers play this tune in D.

St. Anne's Reel

51

La Bastringue

Le Reel du Sucre

Westphalia Waltz

This tune is from the fine fiddling of Louis Beaudoin, *Louis Beaudoin* (Philo 2000). Most of the tunes from his albums work well on the piano accordion.

Westphalia Waltz

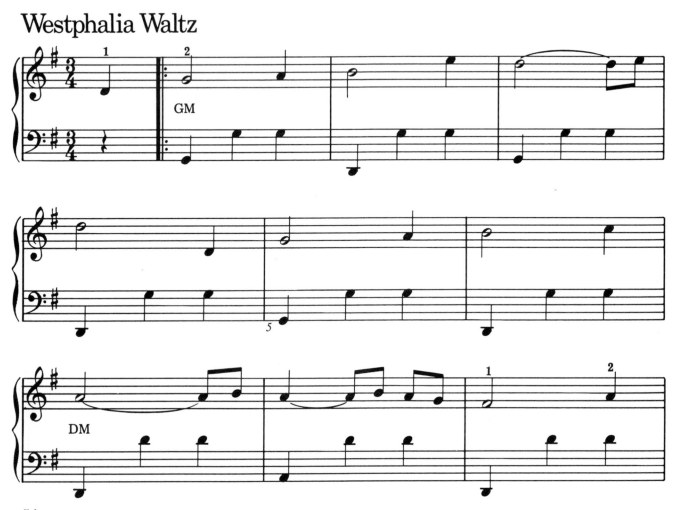

You Married My Daughter (But Yet You Didn't) and Reel de Montréal

These are two G tunes. "You Married My Daughter (But Yet You Didn't)" can be heard on *The Wonderbeans* (Flying Crow FC 101) and "Reel de Montréal" on *La Famille Beaudoin* (Philo 2022). Once you have learned these tunes pick a few phrases at random from each and try to understand the relationship of the phrase to the chord being played. You will notice that most of the notes emphasized are directly from the chord. Other scale tones are used to complement these primary notes of the melody and aid their passing from one phrase to another.

In "You Married My Daughter," the two eighth notes at the beginning of measures 1 and 2 are the primary notes of the melody and the chord. The G chord begins the piece. The notes in the second half of measure 1 form a link between the two eighth note Gs which begin measures 1 and 2. The notes in the second half of measure 2 form a bridge from the G chord to the D chord. Compare these two G chord measures with the next two measures which are played around the D chord. Their patterns are identical with the exception of the notes in the melody which emphasize F♯, the third of the D chord.

You Married My Daughter (But Yet You Didn't)

Reel de Montréal

58

59

La Ringuette

Kate and Lou (Flying Crow FC 105) — piano accordion.

Portrait of Du Vieux Kebec (Opus OP 241) — Jean Marie-Roberge — button accordion.

8va is an abbreviation for octave. When 8va is notated, as it is in the B part of this tune, play these notes one octave higher.

   or

La Ringuette

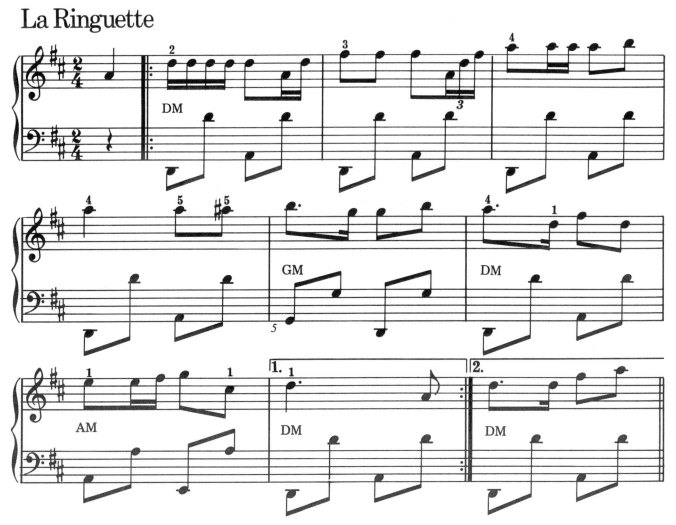

Cajun and Texas-Mexican Tunes
Jole Blonde

Clifton Chenier is a most innovative accordion player. His roots and influence reach into cajun music and blues and his own sounds are always strong whether it be rhythm and blues, cajun blues (zydeco), or Clifton's blues. The cajun blues music of the black cajuns is called zydeco. "Jole Blonde" is one of the most popular cajun tunes and this version is from Clifton Chenier's Arhoolie record *Bon Ton Roulet!* (F 1031). I recommend any of his records (check discography).

Tremolo

A *tremolo* is a rapid trill. It is one of the most effective techniques in blues and is used often on most keyboard instruments. It is notated with the word *trem* followed by a wavy line just above the staff. The amount of tremolo (how quickly you play the alternating notes) is left up to experimentation and your personal taste.

Slow Tremolo

   or

Fast Tremolo

   or

Clifton Chenier

62

Jole Blonde

Arrangement by Clifton Chenier © by Tradition Music Co. (BMI)

Corn Bread Rough

Huddie Ledbetter, better known as Leadbelly, is mostly known for his 12-string guitar playing, but he did record a few sides on the single row, ten-button melodeon. "Corn Bread Rough" works well on the piano accordion and can be heard on *Zydeco* (Arhoolie F 1009).

Corn Bread Rough

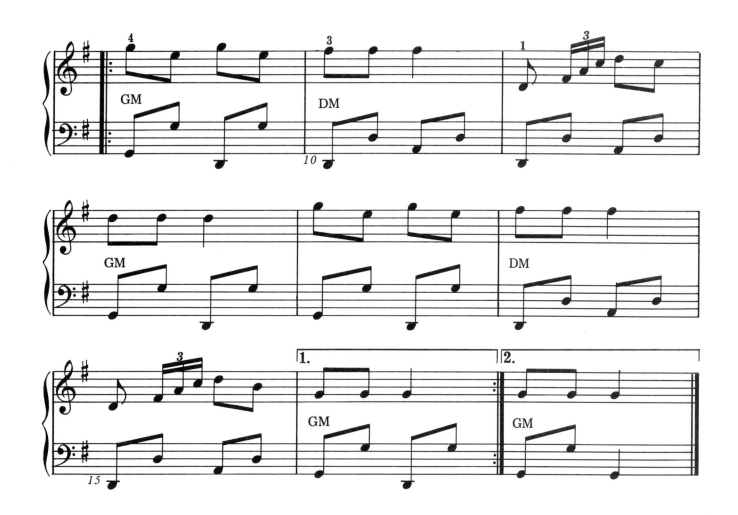

Cajun Two Step

Traditional cajun music was played on a button accordion or a melodeon. These instruments only have a few bass buttons. The bass notes in cajun music are played with a smooth, but heavy touch. Be sure to give your left-hand notes their full time value. The traditional version of this tune can be heard on *Cajun Fais Do-Do* featuring Nathan Abshire and his Pine Grove Boys (Arhoolie F 5004). I play this tune a little slower, almost as a zydeco piece, *Kate and Lou* (Flying Crow FC 105).

Cajun Two Step

Port Arthur Waltz

"Port Arthur Waltz" is a cajun tune from the Balfa Brothers album *J'Ai Vu Le Loup Le Frenard St. La Belette* (Rounder 6007). Try the bass run in measures 7 and 15.

Port Arthur Waltz

La Nopalera

"La Nopalera" is a Texas-Mexican tune from Santiago Jimenez. In Texas-Mexican vocal music the harmony is usually in parallel thirds (see "Chicken Reel Stomp" pg. 46). The A part of this instrumental tune is almost entirely parallel thirds. The notes will flow easily if you use chord positions as your base in selecting the fingering.

G Chord Position

D Chord Position

"La Nopalera" and 15 other great Texas-Mexican border accordion tunes are on *Texas-Mexican Border Music, Vol. 4* (Folklyric Records 9006).

La Nopalera

Flor Marchita

"Flor Marchita" was recorded in San Antonio, Texas in 1937 by Narciso Martinez, *Texas-Mexican Border Music, Vol. 4* (Norteno Accordeon). The A part of this tune reveals a central European influence while the B part has a real Texas-Mexican flavor.

Flor Marchita

Vijando En Polka

I always enjoy the recordings of Flaco Jimenez whether I'm listening to a good solid dance tune such as this polka, a corrido (ballad), or modern sounds backing up Ry Cooder. For a sampling of his button accordion music from 1955 to 1967, listen to *Flaco Jimenez, y su conjunto* (Arhoolie 3007).

Many piano accordion players, especially in commercial music, play with a smooth and gentle touch. Don't be afraid to let your accordion yell. To get a real Texas-Mexican button-accordion sound, pay close attention to the staccato notes and rests.

Flaco Jimenez (left)

Vijando En Polka

Breaks
Hound Dog Baby

Bluesscene USA, The Louisiana Blues (Story-ville SLP 177) includes two accordion tunes. Jay (Mr. Sugar Bee) Stutes features Vorris "Shorty" LeBlanc playing some basic blues riffs on the accordion. Playing the octave D notes in the first measure is still another way to make your squeeze box cry out the blues.

Emphasize the B♭ notes for a bluesy sound.

Hound Dog Baby

Your On My Mind

I learned "Your On My Mind" from a 78 recording by Ted Daffan's Texasans. I have reworked this country and western tune and recorded it in a blues style, *Kate and Lou* (Flying Crow FC 105).

Your On My Mind

Louis and Kate Giampetruzzi

Je vas Revenir (I Will Return)

Je Vas Revenir is another cajun blues (zydeco) tune recorded by Queen Ida. It is difficult sometimes to reproduce exactly a melody or rhythm from button to piano accordion because of the physical differences between the two instruments. I find Queen Ida's choice of notes on her three row button accordion very clean and easily applicable to piano accordion. Queen Ida's *Zydeco* (Crescendo GNP 2101) is one of my favorite records.

Je vas Revenir (I Will Return)

Rufus's Mare

Accordion player Gordon Fleming supports Alan Mills vocals, *Songs of the Maritimes* (Folkways FW 8744) with fine backup accordion. His accordion is played with a light tone register and with its concertina-like melody, "Rufus's Mare" proves to be a perfect setting for Gordon Fleming accordion.

Rufus's Mare

First Born

Aside from being good vocalists, talented song-writers, and versatile musicians Kate and Anna McGarrigle both play button accordion. In "First Born" I do not use an alternating bass. The left hand plays sustained chords.

First Born

Eh 'Tite Fille

If anyone ever tells you the accordion is a limited instrument have them listen to Clifton Chenier. Some people play the accordion with a smooth, soft, gentle touch. In a maritime ballad or a morris dance tune that's fine. However, when playing the blues a smooth touch can add a commercial or pop sound. Clifton Chenier can make his accordion cry, yell, jump or do just about anything he wants. "Eh, 'Tite Fille" makes use of several techniques discussed in this book such as grace notes, blues notes, and triplets. If you need to review them go back to the section where that specific technique was discussed.

Eh 'Tite Fille

Ain't No More Cane

Bob Dylan and The Band recorded this traditional tune and it can be heard on the *Basement Tapes* (Columbia 33682). Garth Hudson's accordion solo at the end of the tune is transcribed here. His solo is full of great blues passages.

Parallel Grace Notes

In measure 8 there are parallel thirds used as grace notes. Your second and fourth fingers should slide from the grace notes to the main notes.

In measure 14 your fourth finger should slide in a similar manner from the A note to the B note.

The Band

86

Ain't No More Cane

Appendices

1. *Everyday Maintenance*—The accordion is a very sensitive instrument. Getting into good everyday habits can save you some repair money in the long run. The biggest enemies of the accordion are dirt, dust, and dampness. Playing outside in damp weather can be harmful for it often causes keys and reeds to stick. It is not advisable to play on the beach or near salt water. I have played gigs under these circumstances and have had keys stick (usually the primary note in the tune I wanted to play).

Always keep a soft cloth in your case for dusting. Be meticulous. Dust your accordion as soon as you are about to put it away. Occasionally check your straps and the hardware which attaches it to your accordion. If the hardware gives way or a strap breaks you may find your accordion on the floor with an expensive repair or irreparable crack. Finally, and probably most important is your case. A good tight case will protect your accordion against both dust and dampness.

2. *Accessories*—Challenger has a complete line of accessories. Their catalog includes shoulder straps, bass straps, an adjustable cross strap (for your back), chest pads, silicone-treated polishing cloths, and a plastic dust cover which enables you to keep your accordion out of its case when at home. If you can't find these items at your local music store write to *Pietro Deiro Music Headquarters*, 133 Seventh Avenue South, New York, N.Y. 10014.

3. *Buying a used accordion*—Accordions can be expensive to repair. Keep this in mind when buying a second hand instrument. Look for something in good working order. Seek advice from someone other than the person you are speaking to about the instrument. Check all the keys and all the buttons. Be sure they all work smoothly and sound clear tones. Listen and look for leaks in the bellows. If all the keys along the fingerboard are not even (in height) someone other than a professional repairman has probably tinkered with the insides of that instrument. Check for evenness in the height of the bass buttons too. Inspect the straps and try the tone registers.

4. *Buying a new accordion*—New accordions just like everything else these days are expensive. Once again seek professional advice from someone other than the person from which you intend to buy the instrument. New accordions can be found for as low as $400 and I've tried some for as high as $3000. It is advisable, if you don't know much about accordions, to choose a standard brand. Hohner, Sonola, Excelsior, and Avanti are just a few.

If you intend to play a lot of French Canadian, Irish, English, or Texas-Mexican music, a good feature to look for is *French Musette* tuning. Different companies have different ways of designing this kind of tuning. It often has a reed tuned lower than pitch, one tuned higher than pitch and one at standard pitch. This combination creates a vibrato effect much like that on the button accordions traditionally used in these styles.

Example — three different A reeds, which all sound at the same time, are tuned as follows:

lower than pitch — A — 437 vibrations per second
standard pitch — A — 440 vibrations per second
higher than pitch — A — 443 vibrations per second

5. *Circle of Fifths* —If you play a series of notes beginning with C ascending in fifths (the fifth degree of the scale), on the twelfth note you will arrive at another C. You will have completed a circle of fifths.

Example — Begin on a C and play all the notes on this chart in a clockwise direction.

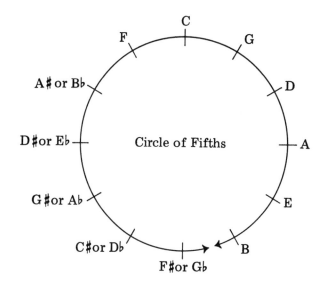

If you play the notes from this chart in a counter-clockwise direction you will have a perfect circle of fourths.

6. *Left-Hand Theory*—The left-hand bass buttons follow this pattern of fifths and fourths. The bass buttons go up (toward the top) in a circle of fifths and down (toward the floor) in a circle of fourths. For a comparison I will unwind the circle of fifths and line it up with the bass buttons. Notice the notes in the circle of fifths (unwound) follow the same pattern as the bass buttons marked.

Circle of Fifths (unwound)

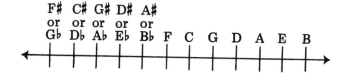

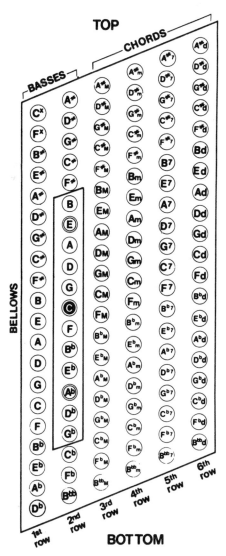

Discography

Some of the tunes in the book are from good accordion records, some are isolated accordion cuts from anthologies, and some are taken from other related sources. I have also listed some additional records which I feel would be good to listen to and some record company addresses.

Roundup Records
Box 474
Somerville, Ma. 02144

Arhoolie and Folklyric Records
Box 9195
Berkeley, Calif. 94709

Topic Records
27 Nassington Road
London NW3 2TX

Folkways Records
43 W. 61st Street
New York, NY 10023

Library of Congress
Recorded Sound Section
Music Division
Washington, D.C. 20540

Flying Crow Records
Box 417, Cathedral Station
New York, NY 10025

Philo Records
The Barn
North Ferrisburg, Vt. 05473

Shanachie Records
1375 Crosby Avenue
Bronx, NY 10461

Front Hall Records
RD 1 Wormer Road
Voorheesville, NY 12186

County Records
P.O. Box 191
Floyd, Va. 24091

Write to these companies for complete catalog listings.

Piano Accordion Records

Robert E. Armstrong, with R. Crumb and his Cheap Suit Serenaders.

R. Crumb and his Cheap Suit Serenaders (Blue Goose 2014), one or two cuts.
R. Crumb and his Cheap Suit Serenaders, Vol. 2 (2019), one or two cuts.
Number Three (2025), one or two cuts.

Christopher Caswell
(Backup)
Journey's Edge, Robin Williamson & His Merry Band (Flying Fish FF 033), three cuts.

Clifton Chenier*
(Cajun Blues)
Louisianna Blues and Zydeco (Arhoolie 1024)
Bon Ton Roulet (1031)
Black Snake Blues (1038)
King of the Bayous (1052)
Live (1059)
Out West (1072)
Bogalusa Boogie (1076)
Clifton Chenier and His Red Hot Louisiana Band (1078)
Bayou Soul (Crazy Cajun 1002)
In New Orleans (GNP Crescendo 2119)
Clifton's Cajun Blues (Prophesy PR-S 1004)

*Clifton Chenier can also be heard on various anthologies.

Joe Cornell
(Big band swing)
Joe Cornell with Duke Ellington (Decca DL 79247), two cuts.

Nick DeCarlo
(Backup)
Rickie Lee Jones (Warner Brothers K-3296)
Kate and Anna McGarrigle (B-2862), one cut.

Gordon Fleming
(Canadian)
Alan Mills (Folkways FW 8744)

Sally Ann Forrester
(Backup bluegrass)
Bill Monroe, 16 All Time Great Hits (Columbia CS 1065), two or three cuts.

Louis Giampetruzzi
(Several Styles)
The Wonderbeans (Flying Crow FC 101), two cuts.
Kate and Lou (FC 105), five or six cuts.

Tony Gumino
(Jazz)
The Best of Willie Smith (GNP Crescendo 2005),
   three or four breaks.

Johnny Handle
(English)
The Collier Lad — with the High Level Ranters
   (Topic 12TS270)
Northumberland For Ever (12TS186)
The Bonny Pit Laddie (2-12TS271/1)
Ranting Lads (12TS297)
Four in a Bar (12TS388)
Johnny Handle (Trailer LER 2007)
Welcome to Cafe Lena (Biograph BLP 12046),
   one or two cuts.

Garth Hudson
(Rock backup and fills)
The Band (Capitol 132)
Cahoots, with The Band (Capitol 651), one or two
   cuts.
Basement Tapes, Bob Dylan and The Band
   (Columbia 33682), one or two cuts.

Ian Holder
(English)
Adieu To Old England, Shirley Collins (Topic
   12TS238)

Dudley Laufman
(Irish, English, and New England music on button
and piano accordion)
Swinging on a Gate (Front Hall FHR 03)
Canterbury Country Dance Orchestra (F&W 3)
Canterbury Orchestra Meets the F&W String Band
   (F&W 4)
Mistwold (F&W 5)

Phyllis McCumby
(Backup bluegrass)
Charlie Bailey and the Happy Valley Boys (Old
   Homestead OHCS 102), one or two cuts.

Bob McQuillen, with Debby McClatchy
(Backup)
Lady Luck (Innisfree/Green Linnet SIF 1017), one
   cut.

Kevin Taylor
(Irish)
Kevin Taylor (Incheronin Inc 7418)

Art Van Damme
(Jazz)
Quintet (Pausa PP 7027)

Blind Connie Williams
(Blues)
Blind Connie Williams (Testament T-2225), two
   cuts.

Button Accordion

Philippe Bruneau
(French Canadian)
Philippe Bruneau (Philo 2003)
Danses pour veillees Canadiennes (2006)

Joe Burke
(Irish)
A Tribute to Michael Coleman (Shaskeen 360)
Traditional Music of Ireland (360)

Link Davis, with Asleep at the Wheel.
(Cajun Style)
Collision Course (Capitol, EMI 11726)

Jimmy Doyle and Dan O'Leary
(Irish)
Traditional Music From the Kingdom of Kerry
   (Shanachie 29007)

Joseph Falcon
(Cajun)
Joseph Falcon (Arhoolie 5005)

Flaco Jimenez
(Folk rock backup)
Chicken Skin Music, Ry Cooder (Reprise 2254)
Showtime, Ry Cooder and the Chicken Skin Revue
   (Warner Brothers B-3059)

Flaco Jimenez
(Texas-Mexican)
y su conjunto (Arhoolie 3007)

John Kirkpatrick and Sue Harris
(English)
The Rose of Britain's Isle (12TS247)
Among the Many Attractions (12TS295)
Shreds and Patches (12TS355)

Queen Ida and the Bon Temps Band
(Zydeco)
Zydeco (GNP Crescendo CRS 2101)
Zydeco à la Mode (CRS 2112)

Kate and Anna McGarrigle
(Folk)
Kate and Anna McGarrigle (Warner Brothers
B-2862)
Dancer with Bruised Knees (3014)

Anthologies (accordion and other related albums
including at least one tune with accordion, piano,
or button)

Folklyric
Norteno Accordeon (9006)*
Norteno Accordeon part 2 (9019)*
Norteno Accordeon part 3 (9020)*

Arhoolie
Zydeco (1009)
Chulas Fronteras (3005)
Cajun Fais Do-Do (5004)
Nathan Abshire and Other Cajun Gems (5013)

Topic
Northumbrian Country Music (12TS267)
Melodeon Greats (12TS376)

String
Beer Parlor Jive (801)

Opus
Portrait of Du Vieux Kebec (OP241)

Storyville
Bluesscene USA (SLP 177)

Biograph
Welcome to Cafe Lena (BLP 12046)

Library of Congress
Reels, Polkas and More (LBC 4)

Fiddle and String Band Records

Louis Beaudoin (Philo 2000)
La Famille Beaudoin (Philo 2022)

Alan Block and Ralph Lee Smith (Meadowlands 01)

Holy Modal Rounders (Fantasy 24711)

Fire on the Mountain, Highwoods String Band
(Rounder 0023)
J'Ai Vu Le Loup, Le Frenard St. La Belette, The
Balfa Brothers (Rounder 6007)

*All three on *Texas-Mexican Border Music,* various volumes.
Check other volumes.